THE SECOND WORLD
IN PHOTOGRAPHS

1942

THE SECOND WORLD WAR AT SEA IN PHOTOGRAPHS

1942

PHIL CARRADICE

AMBERLEY

First published 2015

Amberley Publishing
The Hill, Stroud
Gloucestershire, GL5 4EP

www.amberley-books.com

British Library Cataloguing in Publication Data.
A catalogue record for this book is available from the British Library.

ISBN 978 1 4456 2249 1 (print)
ISBN 978 1 4456 2272 9 (ebook)

Typeset in 10pt on 12pt Sabon.
Typesetting and Origination by Amberley Publishing.
Printed in the UK.

Contents

Introduction

If the year 1941 had, overall, been one of trauma for Britain, at least by its close there was the consolation of knowing that the country would no longer have to fight alone. After her surprise attack on Pearl Harbor in December 1941, Japan may have joined Germany and Italy in an axis of totalitarian power but the Allied cause was now greatly aided by the military and industrial might of the USSR and the USA.

In the long run, as most astute commentators and politicians realised, such power as Russia and America could bring to the conflict would almost inevitably lead to an Allied victory.

As if to underline the point, at the Arcadia Conference in Washington on 1 January twenty-six nations agreed to combine their efforts and resources in order to defeat the Axis powers.

Just a few days later President Roosevelt proposed a budget to fund 8 million tons of shipping – along with thousands of tanks, aircraft and other vehicles – by the end of 1943. Slowly but surely the economic strength of the USA was being brought into play.

Victory, however, was still a long way ahead when 1942 dawned, and the submarine war continued unabated. America began to understand the problem when the U-boats started to sink large numbers of merchantmen off the east coast of the country. Cities like New York were not blacked out and navigation buoys were lit up like Christmas trees. There were no anti-submarine defences in place and for the U-boat commanders and their crews it was a second 'Happy Time'.

By February the U-boats had expanded their field of operations to the Caribbean, where thousands of tons of Allied and neutral shipping was soon heading to the bottom of the sea. It would take time for the Americans to understand and grasp the significance of the U-boat problem, something that was surprising as for some time they had been seeing, at first hand, the effects of the attacks on British convoys to and from the USA.

Ultimately, it was naïvety on the part of the Americans, a belief that – despite the Pearl Harbour attack – they were blessed with a degree of invulnerability that other nations did not possess. It was an attitude that would take time to dispel.

At the beginning of February the German battlecruisers *Scharnhorst* and *Gneisenau*, along with the heavy cruiser *Prinz Eugen*, made what has been referred to as the 'Channel Dash' from Brest – where they had been holed up for over a year – back to their home base in Germany.

The sudden sortie took everyone by surprise and it was not until mid-morning on 12 February, several hours after they had left port, that the British defences were even aware that the two battlecruisers were on the move. By then it was too late – the German squadron was almost through the Dover Strait.

As one London newspaper ruefully reported, the Germans had done what the Duke of Medina Sidonia, commander of the Spanish Armada, had failed to do in 1588 and successfully traversed the Channel. Hurriedly organised British attacks using land-based aircraft, coastal artillery and motor torpedo boats led only to the loss of forty-two aircraft.

Escorted by over 100 smaller vessels, as well as dozens of aircraft under the command of Adolf Galland, the Channel Dash was a remarkable achievement and although the *Scharnhorst* suffered damage after hitting a mine when she was almost home, the Royal Navy and the RAF had proved to be powerless to prevent the enemy ships making port.

Further disaster came on 15 February when Singapore, Britain's largest base in the Far East, capitulated to the Japanese. General Percival surrendered the base along with 138,000 men. Japanese losses during the campaign had been less than 10,000.

As if that was not enough, on 27 February came the Battle of the Java Sea. A combined Dutch, British, American and Australian force under the command of Rear Admiral Karel Doorman attempted to intercept a Japanese squadron escorting the invasion fleet bound for Java. The battle, the largest ship-to-ship engagement since Jutland in 1916, was a disaster for the Allies. The Dutch cruisers *De Ruyter* and *Java* were sunk, the *Exeter* badly damaged and Rear Admiral Doorman killed.

The following day, the Australian cruiser *Perth* and the American *Houston* were sunk in the Sunda Straits. On 1 March, as she limped towards Ceylon (Sri Lanka), the *Exeter*, one of the victors of the Battle of the River Plate, was hunted down by the more powerful Japanese cruisers and also sunk. The battles delayed the invasion of Java but by the beginning of March the inevitable had happened and the Japanese had landed on the island.

The war in Europe continued badly with highlights such as the commando raid on Saint-Nazaire, despite the deaths of many of the attacking soldiers in the operation, being hailed in the British newspapers as an example of glorious sacrifice. The delayed explosion of ammunition on the old four-stacker *Campbeltown* which had rammed the dock gates meant that the operation was at least partly successful.

The Malta convoys continued, at a terrible cost to men of the Merchant Marine, and in April the besieged island of Malta was awarded the George Cross, the first time such a medal had been awarded to a corporate body rather than an individual. It was undoubtedly a well-deserved accolade but the men of the Merchant Navy could have been excused for wondering what they had to do to gain some type of recognition.

The tide of war began to change when, on 7 May, an American fleet encountered a Japanese force at the Battle of the Coral Sea, the action effectively removing the threat of an invasion of Australia. It was the first time that a major ship action had ever been fought where the major vessels never actually saw each other, all of the damage being inflicted by carrier-borne aircraft.

Although the Americans actually suffered greater ship losses – the aircraft carrier *Lexington* being a major casualty – the battle was a strategic victory for the USA. Of particular importance was the severe damage inflicted on the Japanese fleet carriers *Shōkaku* and *Zuikaku*, which were forced to return to base for repairs. As a consequence they missed the next, vitally important action in the Pacific sea war.

The victory at the Coral Sea was followed up less than a month later when, in a series of related actions between 4 and 7 June, the Americans fought and won the Battle of Midway. It was a wide, sprawling battle that – because of its consequences – was, arguably, the most significant naval action of the whole war.

Admiral Yamamoto had been hoping to lure the American carrier fleet into a trap by launching an attack on Midway Island but Allied code breakers had managed to crack the Japanese codes and, as a result, the American admirals Nimitz, Spruance and Fletcher were able to reverse the surprise and inflict serious losses on the enemy. The battle consisted, in the main, of carrier-borne aircraft attacking enemy ships and planes, with very little scope for big-gun warship action.

The use of aircraft rather than battleships did not prevent major damage being inflicted on the Japanese fleet. In fact, so serious was the damage, with four aircraft carriers and one heavy cruiser sunk, that the losses were irreversible and truly did have a major impact on the course and outcome of the Pacific war.

The second half of 1942 was not all success for the Allies, however. In July, Convoy PQ 17 to Russia was decimated after the First Sea Lord, Admiral Dudley Pound – faced by the threat of the *Tirpitz* and other capital ships – ordered the ships to scatter, thus placing them at the mercy of German U-boats and aircraft.

Only eleven merchant vessels out of a total of thirty-six survived the ordeal, thousands of vehicles, tanks and planes going down with the merchantmen. Despite the disaster, the Russian convoys continued to run, several of them suffering heavy losses that were almost on a par with PQ 17.

On 8 November Allied troops landed in North Africa, Operation Torch as it was known. Although US Marines had landed on Guadalcanal in the Pacific some months before, this was the first time US troops had taken the offensive in the European theatre of war. It was a combined operation by British, Commonwealth and American troops, effectively encircling the German armies fighting along the North African coast.

The year had been a long and bitter one, with huge casualties on all sides. But by the end of 1942 it was clear that the tide was finally turning – the war was not yet won but, to mis-quote Churchill, it was the end of the beginning in the long march to victory.

January

President Roosevelt is seen here signing the declaration of war against Japan. On 7 January 1942 he proposed a budget that had a clear war aim – to find, by the end of 1943, sufficient money to build and launch 8 million tons of shipping along with many thousands of military vehicles and aircraft. The proposal was accepted.

Above left: This photograph shows Japanese warships ready for action. Note the catapult aircraft waiting on the deck of one of the ships.

Above right: In a brief but bloodthirsty action off Mindanao, British forces clashed with Japanese raiders. One Japanese destroyer was sunk in the action.

Below: Anti-aircraft gunners stand ready and alert, waiting for aerial attack.

The *U-123* is shown here in her home port, crew lined up on her deck. On 12 January 1942 she became one of the first U-boats to achieve success off the American coast when she sank a steamer within a few miles of New York.

It took time but, eventually, the Americans began to realise that ports along the Eastern Seaboard like New York and Boston would have to be 'blacked out'. American destroyers were added to the British convoy escorts.

Communication between escorts and merchant ships in a convoy was always difficult. This photograph shows a signalman on board a destroyer flashing a message to a merchant ship. The same message might have to be repeated a dozen times.

A U-boat has been forced to the surface, her crew swimming for their lives in the water.

Survivors from a sunken
merchantman cling to the keel
of their upturned lifeboat.

Escorts and merchantman are shown here under attack. Bombs rain down from the hidden enemy
aircraft.

A British submarine setting out on patrol.

Anti-submarine patrols were mounted by a whole variety of warships. This photograph shows a drifter which was one of many small craft drafted into service in 1941/42.

Minesweeping trawlers in the North Sea.

On 30 January the submarine *Thorn* sank the Italian submarine *Medua* in the Mediterranean. It was one of many British successes in Mussolini's 'Italian Lake'.

Officers and men of the submarine *Tigris*, a vessel which operated mainly in Russian waters.

The carrier *Victorious* is shown here, turned into the wind, ready to land aircraft. Some of those aircraft can be seen in the sky above the ship.

Construction of British capital ships continued throughout the war. It obviously took longer to build a battleship than an escort vessel, but the fleet had to be kept up-to-date. This shows the brand new battleship *Duke of York*.

Cramped and uncomfortable it might be, but ratings on a British submarine still manage to enjoy tea-time. The atmosphere, with cigarette smoke and cooking fumes mixing with diesel, could not have been particularly pleasant.

February

A submarine gun crew on deck – the fresh air would have been as welcome as anything else.

Convoys to Malta were essential to keep the island supplied during the siege by Italian and German naval and aerial forces. This photograph shows the safe arrival of a convoy at Malta in the early days of 1942.

From the days of the Napoleonic Wars, sea forts and Martello Towers had been an important part of the defence of the British shore line. The Second World War was no different. This photograph shows a fort on the South Coast.

This photograph shows the gun crew in the fort. It must have been a lonely and sometimes depressing posting.

A launch carrying supplies out to the fort.

In the early days of 1942, Japanese forces raged triumphantly across the Far East and Pacific. On 2 February their forces landed on the Bataan Peninsula.

A Japanese naval reconnaissance plane complete with pilot on the wing – aerial supremacy was a crucial factor in Japanese success.

On 11/12 February the German battlecruisers *Scharnhorst* and *Gneisenau* sortied out from Brest, making a run for their home port in Germany. A Fairey Swordfish aircraft, complete with torpedo, is seen here out to attempt an interception. Slow and unwieldy, the Swordfish aircraft made many highly effective attacks during the war but they were largely ineffective during the 'Channel Dash'.

Blenheim pilots after the disappointing and failed attacks on the *Scharnhorst* and *Gneisenau* during the Channel Dash. British forces were unable to prevent the two battlecruisers from making the run and forty-two British aircraft were lost attempting to intercept the German ships.

An aerial view of the harbour and dock installations at Kiel. The *Gneisenau* is clearly visible in the floating dock, undergoing repairs for damage sustained during the Channel Dash.

The war in the North Atlantic continued, sometimes in treacherous and dangerous conditions. This shows a vessel in Arctic waters.

The danger of capsizing was ever-present when ice formed on the deck and rigging of ships. Chipping the ice off equipment was a hated but necessary task for all sailors.

The destroyer *Campbell* launches her torpedoes.

The minesweeper *Britmart*, which shot down an attacking Ju 88.

Survivors from a sunken merchantman are shown here on their life raft.

Singapore surrendered to the Japanese on 15 February 1942. It was major humiliation for the British as the fortress and city had been considered invincible. The British lost 138,000 men in the campaign, the Japanese fewer than 10,000. This shows Lt General Percival, led by a Japanese officer, marching into captivity.

Fairey Fulmar aircraft of the Royal Fleet Air Arm.

Fairey Albacores taking off from HMS *Victorious*. The battleship *King George V* is ahead of her.

The Battle of the Java Sea took place on 27 February. A combined Dutch, Australian, British and American fleet under Admiral Karel Doorman ran into a superior Japanese force and was destroyed in the largest ship-to-ship engagement since the Battle of Jutland. This shows Japanese bombs falling close to the Dutch cruiser *Java* which, along with the *De Ruyter*, was sunk in the battle. Doorman was killed.

Rear Admiral Karel Doorman, who died when his flagship *De Ruyter* was sunk during the disastrous Battle of the Java Sea.

HMS *Exeter* under attack during the Battle of the Java Sea. She was severely damaged but managed to limp away.

The day after the Battle of the Java Sea, the Australian cruiser *Perth* (shown here), along with the USS *Houston*, was also sunk.

Landing craft returning home after a raid on the German radio post at Bruneval, north of Le Havre, on 27/28 February. The raid was made in conjunction with parachute troops, one of the first instances of British combined operations.

Commandos and parachutists retiring after the raid on Bruneval.

March

On 1 March, badly damaged and attempting to make port in Ceylon (Sri Lanka), the *Exeter* was intercepted by Japanese heavy cruisers and sunk – a sad end for one of the heroines of the Battle of the River Plate.

A US cruiser fires at invading Japanese forces on the Gilbert and Marshall Islands.

Fairey Albacores taking off from the flight deck of HMS *Formidable*.

On 9 March Albacores from HMS *Victorious* launched an unsuccessful raid against the *Tirpitz*. It was just one of many attacks to be made against the German battleship in the coming years.

Every available ship was needed to fight. The *Thetis* had been sunk at Moelfre on her maiden voyage in 1939. Raised and re-commissioned, she was given the new name *Thunderbolt* and served in the Mediterranean until she was sunk again in 1943.

Trawlers and drifters were ideal vessels for the delicate art of minesweeping. Most of them had wooden hulls and were therefore less likely to set off the German magnetic mines. This shows the crew of a minesweeper at work – in pre-war days she operated as a herring drifter.

Canada, like all of the Colonial and Dominion powers, lent her support to the mother country. This shows a Canadian Flower class corvette patrolling in heavy seas.

Ice on a corvette in the Northern Atlantic.

A British submarine at sea.

Above: Carrying supplies was an essential task in wartime. Even Royal Navy ships were called on to play their part in transporting vital stores and equipment.

Below: Keeping watch on a patrolling destroyer, the pom-pom anti-aircraft guns clearly visible.

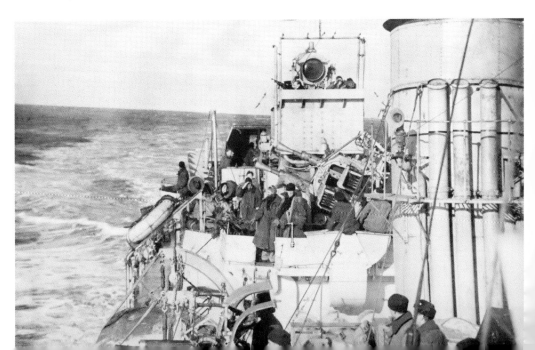

German U-boat survivors, their submarine depth charged to destruction, are shown here being hauled on aboard a British destroyer.

The American tanker *Gulftrade* was one of many US merchant ships sunk off the coast of New York and New Jersey during the early part of 1942. Although she went down just 3 miles off shore, only sixteen of her crew were saved.

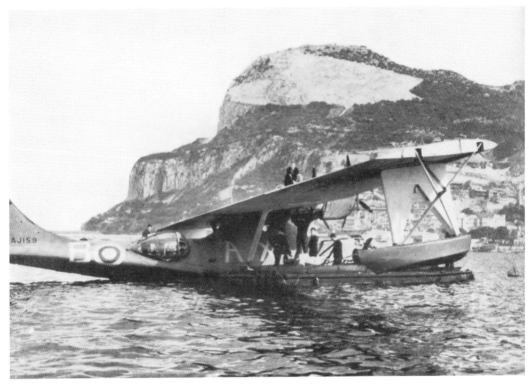

As the war progressed, more and more use was made of aircraft to locate enemy submarines. This photograph shows a Catalina flying boat off Gibraltar.

On the night of 14/15 March 1942, German E-boats and British MTBs clashed in the English Channel. Vessels on both sides were sunk. This photograph shows a Motor Torpedo Boat at sea.

Whitley bombers are shown here above MTBs operating at speed.

Conditions on board the MTBs – and on the German E-boats – were uncomfortable and dangerous. The boats were made of wood and offered little protection from machine gun bullets and cannon shells. This photograph shows a gunner on a British MTB.

The second Battle of Sirte took place on 22 March 1942. Admiral Philip Vian and his force of five cruisers and destroyers repulsed an attack by Italian forces on a Malta convoy. Despite his success, the convoy suffered great losses the following day when it was attacked by Italian and German aircraft. This photograph shows Admiral Vian with American Admiral 'Bull' Halsey later in the war.

A stern view of the battleship *Queen Elizabeth*, flag ship of Admiral Cunningham and the Mediterranean Fleet. It shows the ship's colours being raised first thing in the morning.

The Italian submarine *Anmiraglio Millo* which was sunk by a British submarine off the southern coast of Italy.

The old and the new: aircraft and battleships at sea.

The forward 14-inch guns of the *Duke of York*.

The *Duke of York* fires her guns.

A crashed aircraft is shown here on the deck of an aircraft carrier. Sailors and airmen are watching the rescue operation.

The crew of the submarine *Utmost* are seen here with their traditional Jolly Roger flag showing missions and cruises undertaken. The submarine had sunk several enemy ships and damaged a German cruiser. The knives on the home-made flag represent 'Cloak and Dagger' missions undertaken by the submarine.

German U-boats operated, almost without hindrance, in the Caribbean for several months in the early part of 1942. This photograph shows an unexploded torpedo on the island of Aruba. Later, after the photograph was taken, the torpedo exploded, killing four of the Marines who were trying to make it safe.

An oil tanker ablaze off the island of Curaçao.

On 28 March, the British launched a raid on the dock at Saint-Nazaire. An old four-stacker, *Campbeltown*, was adapted (losing two of her funnels) and driven into the dock gates. Sometime after the raid had finished, explosives on the ship were detonated and serious damage was caused.

An artist's impression of the British naval and commando raid on the dockyard at Saint-Nazaire.

An aerial photograph of Saint-Nazaire after the raid. The numbers indicate the outer dock gate (1), the pump house (2), the machine house (3), sheds (4), fire bays (5), submarine pens (6) and various buildings (7).

The raid on Saint-Nazaire was hailed as a great success but many casualties were incurred. This photograph shows British commandoes taken prisoner during the raid being marched away by German soldiers.

April

On 5 April, the heavy cruisers *Cornwall* and *Dorsetshire* were sunk by Japanese carrier-borne aircraft off the Maldives. Over the next few days the Japanese went on to sink twenty-three merchant vessels in the area. This photograph shows the *Cornwall* in happier times.

Survivors from the *Dorsetshire* in the water after the sinking. Approximately 1,000 survivors from the two ships were picked up by escorting destroyers.

By the beginning of 1942, Japanese successes against unprotected battleships had made everyone aware that the balance of power in sea warfare had shifted away from large capital ships to aircraft. This photograph shows a US dive bomber in the air above its carrier.

The aircraft carrier *Hermes* was sunk off Trincomalee on 9 April when she was attacked by Japanese aircraft – the British had still not learned the value of effective air cover for capital warships.

Aircraft on the forward flight deck of HMS *Hermes*.

Hitler, accompanied by Admiral Raeder, commander of the German Navy, is shown here on a visit to the German fleet. Despite the seeming harmony of the photograph, by the spring of 1942 Hitler was becoming dissatisfied by the performance of his surface fleet. In future more emphasis would be placed on the U-boats.

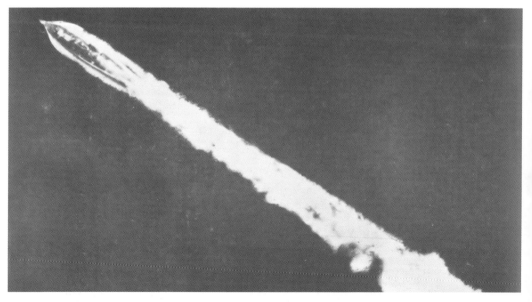

The battleship *Tirpitz*, sister ship to the *Bismarck*, was a constant threat as far as British naval planners were concerned. If she had managed to get out among the Russian convoys, she would have caused untold damage. This aerial view shows her heading at full speed up the fjord at Trondheim.

Above: Another aerial view of the *Tirpitz*. Note the anti-torpedo boom around the ship.

Below left: A British submarine leaves her depot ship to head out on patrol.

Below right: The siege of Malta was a long-drawn-out affair, the island being pummelled by German and Italian bombers. Even so the navy continued to use Malta as a base, particularly for its submarine fleet. On 15 April 1942 Malta was awarded the George Cross, the first time such an award had been made to a corporate body rather than an individual.

Destroyers patrol around a Malta convoy.

Smoke screens were used to confuse enemy aircraft and submarines. This shows one being laid around a Malta convoy.

The smoke of exploding bombs can be clearly seen in this photograph of a raid on Malta.

The island of Malta – and in particular the main town of Valetta – suffered dreadfully from the bombing raids. This shows damage in the main street of the town.

A rather fanciful artist's impression of an air raid on Malta. Ju 88s and Me 110s dive and unleash their bombs on the island. The painting owes more to propaganda than it does to reality.

Mines being dropped over the stern of a mine-layer.

Lt Commander David Wanklyn, recently awarded the Victoria Cross, died when his submarine *Upholder* failed to return to Malta after a patrol in April. He is shown here with his First Lieutenant, J. R. D. Drummond, ashore on the island.

Aircraft come in to land on the flight deck of HMS *Illustrious*. The crew man in the foreground of the picture is controlling the landing process.

An aerial view of HMS *Illustrious* with Swordfish aircraft on her deck.

The cruiser *Edinburgh* was torpedoed by *U-456* in the Barents Sea on 30 April. She was carrying 465 gold bars, which went down with her. Over 430 of these bars were salvaged in 1981.

A lookout on board a Tribal class destroyer keeps a careful watch for enemy U-boats and aircraft.

May

An MTB at sea, patrolling the coastal waters in the English Channel.

On 5 May 1924, British forces landed on the Vichy French island of Madagascar. It was a strategic move as if the island had fallen to the Japanese it could have represented a threat to British supply routes to India. French opposition to the British landings was limited, just one submarine and a sloop being sunk.

The Battle of the Coral Sea was fought on 6/7 May 1942. This shows the Japanese carrier *Ryukaku* exploding after a torpedo hit from American planes in the early stages of the action. Although they lost more ships, the battle was a strategic victory for the Americans.

An official portrait of Admiral Chester W. Nimitz, who became C-in-C of the US Pacific Fleet on the last day of 1941. Later in 1942, he would be appointed C-in-C Pacific Ocean Areas, with command over all Allied units there.

A sentry stands on a torpedo boat under construction in a US shipyard.

A US Navy gunner in an aircraft at the naval air station at Corpus Christi, Texas.

A US Navy Consolidated Catalina flying boat at the naval air station at Corpus Christi, Texas.

A mechanic works on an engine of one of the PBY Catalina flying boats at Corpus Christi.

US Marines working with a barrage balloon on Parris Island, South Carolina.

A trainee Marine glider pilot sits in his cockpit, watching the take-offs, at Page Field on Parris Island, South Carolina.

A crowd of workers leaving the Pennsylvania shipyards, Beaumont, Texas.

A poster warning captains to avoid making smoke that might attract enemy submarines.

STUDENTEN

SEID
PROPA-
GANDISTEN
DES
FÜHRERS

HOCH-u.FACHSCHULEN BEKENNEN SICH AM 29.MÄRZ
ZUR DEUTSCHEN FREIHEITSBEWEGUNG

A German poster encouraging students to become more involved with the Nazi Party.

When the Stukas begin to attack
Ain't the time to make up for a lack
Of cleaning your gun —
Which won't shoot at a Hun
With a month's gummy dust on its back!

CLEAN IT EVERY 3 DAYS

Don't be a dope! **HANDLE EQUIPMENT RIGHT**

A Joe Dope poster by Will Eisner encouraging US servicemen to look after their equipment properly.

Arms for Russia: a convoy sails into Murmansk under the protective umbrella of Soviet fighters.

The end of the *Lexington*, with crew leaping over the side of the ship.

After the fall of France in 1940, Hitler allowed the rump of the French state to establish itself as Vichy France. This photograph shows Marshal Petain and Admiral Darlan of the Vichy government inspecting the battleship *Dunkerque* at Toulon.

"I'm sorry, but I can't train the
home in five inches of wat

Above left: Making smoke, one of the important tactics used during the war.

Above right: 'Total War', a cartoon from 1942.

Sir Percy Noble, C-in-C Western Approaches, talks to an RAF officer.

A German Heinkel He 111 bomber. On 27 May a formation of these aircraft, along with a number of Ju 88s, attacked convoy PQ 16. Seven freighters were lost in the attack.

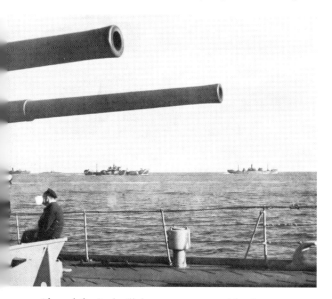

Above left: And still the convoys go on. Merchantmen are seen here from the deck of an escorting cruiser.

Above right: Unheralded but necessary work, one of the aircrew of HMS *Illustrious* carrying shells to the guns.

H.M.S RAMILLIES

H.M.S. ROYAL SOVEREIGN.

H.M.S. REVENGE.

BATTLESHIPS RETURNING HOME
AFTER EXERCISES.   38B-11

Small two-man human torpedos and tiny midget submarines were a new weapon of war.

Opposite: On 30 May the battleship *Ramillies*, shown here in line behind the *Royal Sovereign* and *Revenge*, was severely damaged by a Japanese midget submarine at Diego Suarez.

The crew of the submarine *Upright* are shown here after returning from patrol, proudly displaying their Jolly Roger.

The British submarine *Thunderbolt*, one of an increasing number of submarines used by the Royal Navy.

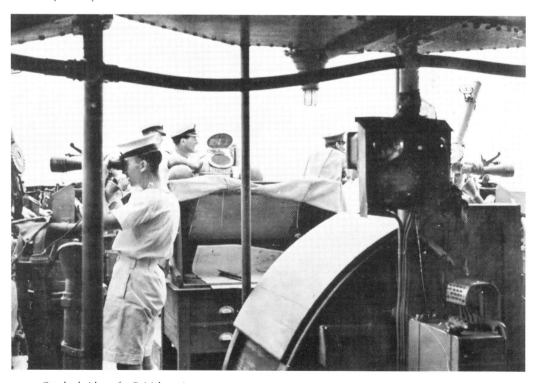

On the bridge of a British cruiser.

HMS *Penelope* enters the Grand Harbour at Malta. Even when she had made harbour and could be considered safe, the cruiser was given no respite, being attacked every day for the two weeks she was in port.

British battleships remained a significant threat to all of the Axis powers throughout the war years.

June

The Battle of Midway was perhaps the major naval action of the whole war. This shows the US carrier *Yorktown* fighting off Japanese dive bombers during the early stages of the battle.

Above: By defeating the Japanese at Midway, American forces ensured ultimate victory for the Allies. The battle was predominantly fought by carrier-borne aircraft, operating over the vast empty stretches of the Pacific. US Navy Dauntless dive bombers from the carrier *Hornet* played a vital role in the action.

Below: Devastator bombers are shown here on the flight deck of USS *Yorktown* during the Battle of Midway. Several of them still have their wings folded.

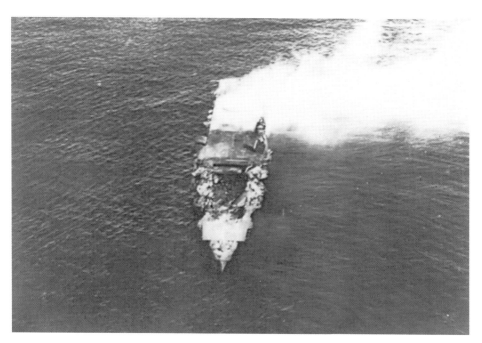

Four Japanese aircraft carriers were sunk during the battle. This photograph shows the *Hiryū* on fire and drifting before she finally slips below the waves.

While the aircraft carriers of both sides were the principal targets, it was also important to destroy surface craft. The Japanese cruiser *Mikuma* was a victim of several air attacks, being battered into submission before sinking.

The USS *Yorktown* was a symbol of American strength and power, as important to the American public as the *Ark Royal* was to the British.

Crippled by Japanese bombs, the *Yorktown* was left helpless in the water. It was obvious to everyone that she was sinking.

Smoke billows from the centre castle and deck of the *Yorktown* as crewmen worked to save the stricken ship – in vain.

Aircraft carriers were, in reality, little more than floating aerodromes but they were a vital component in any navy.

Above: The USS *Hammann* was one of the few ships not sunk by aerial attack during the Battle of Midway. The Japanese submarine *I-168* had approached the American fleet unsuspected and fired a torpedo at the *Hammann* before anybody realised the danger.

Right: An anti-aircraft gun crew – anti-aircraft weapons were of vital importance in keeping ships safe.

US anti-aircraft gunners on the deck of their ship.

Above: Escorts and merchantmen for convoy PQ 17 assemble in Hvalfjord, Iceland. This photograph shows the destroyer *Icarus* and, behind her, a Russian oil tanker. At this stage nobody suspected the tragedy that was to come.

Right: An aerial view of the *Gneisenau.* The letters A, B and C indicate the ship's dismantled eleven-inch gun turrets. D shows camouflage over her stern, E the base of the gun turrets and F the ball bearings that enable the turrets to turn.

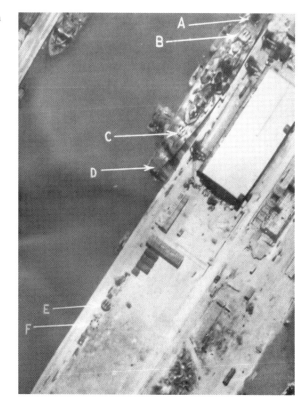

A stern view of a British destroyer in the Mediterranean.

Opposite above: Sir Percy Noble addresses the crew of HMS *Stork*, which had recently sunk the *U-574*.

Opposite below: This shows the crew of the minesweeper *Northern Sky*. Before the war, she had been a Grimsby trawler.

Hoisting 15-inch shells onto the battleship *Warspite*.

Defending troop convoys was an important part of the Navy's work. This shows soldiers disembarking from their troop ship in Egypt.

Submarines were the unseen killers of the war. Very often, the first thing a ship's crew knew of their presence was a torpedo exploding against their hull. This shows a torpedo being loaded onto a British submarine.

On 30 June, the depot ship *Medway* was torpedoed and sunk off Alexandria. Her cargo of ninety torpedoes and spare machinery went down with her.

July

Despite freezing conditions, on 1 July German reconnaissance aircraft located convoy PQ 17 as it ploughed towards Murmansk. On 2 July the *Tirpitz*, *Admiral Hipper* and a number of destroyers left Trondheim to intercept the convoy. They were soon joined by the *Admiral Scheer* and the *Lützow*.

Faced by seemingly impossible
odds, Admiral Dudley Pound,
First Sea Lord, ordered the convoy
to scatter and gave instructions
for the escorts to withdraw.
Everyone, he believed, would
have a better chance of survival
by sailing independently rather
than in a convoy. Unfortunately,
the tactic exposed convoy PQ 17
to the full brunt of U-boat and
aeroplane attack.

The USS *Wichita*, one of the escorts for PQ 17.

Admiral Tovey later claimed that Pound's order to scatter the convoy was 'nothing more than sheer bloody murder'. On 5 July alone the convoy lost seventeen ships, mainly to U-boats. On 7 July another eight ships were lost.

Weather conditions on the Russian convoys were appalling, with snow and ice constantly threatening to capsize ships.

Think Home Guard and you immediately think of *Dad's Army*. Not quite true – this photograph shows the Windermere Home Guard patrolling the lake in speed boats.

The demand for aircraft carriers was greater than the shipyards could deliver. Consequently merchant vessels were often converted into temporary carriers. This photograph shows an American conversion.

The carrier *Formidable*, one of many British carriers in service during 1942.

On board a Free French destroyer, with the 5.5-inch guns being clearly shown.

British battleships at sea.

Opposite: A Free French destroyer is shown here dropping depth charges on an enemy submarine.

On the bridge of HMS *Warspite*.

American troops land on Guadalcanal.

August

On 2 August 1942, the *Queen Mary* and *Queen Elizabeth* began transporting American troops across the Atlantic, ready for an eventual invasion of Europe. This shows *Queen Elizabeth* in wartime colours picking up soldiers at Cape Town.

MONTAGUE·B·BLACK

The carrier *Eagle* was sunk off Majorca during Operation Pedestal.

Opposite: The Operation Pedestal convoy to Malta was protected by battleships, carriers, cruisers and thirty-two destroyers. Although the convoy got through to Malta, it was not without cost – the carrier *Eagle*, the cruiser *Manchester* and a number of freighters were sunk in almost constant attacks.

Survivors from the aircraft carrier *Eagle* are shown here being picked up by a British destroyer.

A dramatic photograph of the sinking *Yorktown*, with canting deck and sailors hurriedly abandoning the ship.

A victim of war. A tanker, mined in the English Channel, is run ashore before she sinks.

Flower class corvettes on escort duty in the Atlantic.

The beach at Dieppe after the Allied raid on 19 August 1942. Over 3,000 men were killed or captured and many aircraft and ships were destroyed but valuable lessons were learned about attacking fixed, land-based positions.

September

US Marines landed on Guadalcanal on 8 September 1942. It was the first American amphibious landing of the war and was the beginning of a long, bitterly fought campaign, but it was a start.

British battleships in a heavy sea.

U-boat prisoners, dismayed and disgruntled after their submarine had been rammed and sunk by the corvette *Dianthus*.

German E-boats leave their base for a raid on shipping in the English Channel – E-boat Alley, as the straits were known. The contests between E-boats and British MTBs in the Channel and along the North Sea coast saw some of the bitterest fighting of the whole war.

The need for air cover, for convoys and for independently operating capital ships, had become obvious by 1942. Escort carriers – little more than floating flight platforms – were soon rolling off the stocks in dockyards across Britain and America. This photograph shows one such ship.

A new aircraft carrier slides into the water. Built and launched in the US Navy yard of the Bethlehem Steel Company, Massachusetts, this emergency-built carrier was one of many built during the war years.

Opposite: A torpedo is being fitted to the underside of a Swordfish aircraft by armourers and aircrew.

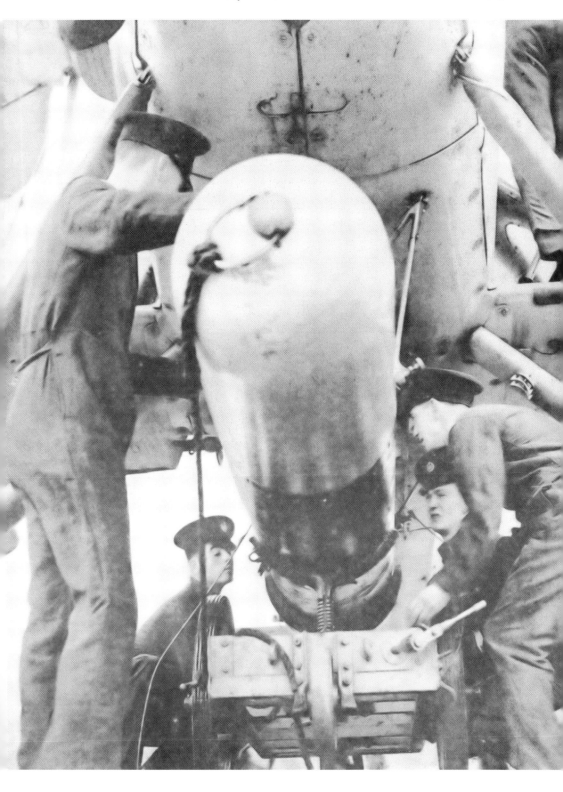

Pom-pom guns on the carrier *Illustrious*.

Opposite above: The *Laconia* was sunk by *U-156* near Ascension Island on 12 September. Carrying over 2,000 troops and POWs, she went quickly to the bottom. In a wonderful humanitarian gesture, Korvettenkapitän Werner Hartenstein, commander of the *U-156*, immediately broadcast the location of the survivors so that any shipping in the area could come to their rescue.

Opposite below: The *U-156* and *U-506* attempting to rescue some of the crew of the *Laconia*. The two U-boats came under aerial attack from a US Liberator, as a result of which Admiral Dönitz issued the Laconia Order forbidding any further humanitarian rescue attempts.

A Sunderland flying boat, which was used for long-range reconnaissance and anti-submarine patrols.

Damage to the conning tower of the Italian submarine *Cobralto*.

October

A British battleship at sea.

There were very few places to lie down on board a submarine and the crew were invariably forced to catch their sleep as and when they could – as this postcard shows.

This artist-drawn card shows a British submarine on the surface at night. Coming to the surface enabled the submarine to recharge her batteries and give the crew a little fresh air.

On 2 October 1942, the liner *Queen Mary* was involved in a collision with the cruiser *Curacoa* while transporting troops across the Atlantic. Sailing at full speed, the *Queen Mary* sliced through the warship. Many of those on board the liner did not know that they had hit anything, and the only damage was a few bent plates.

The *Curacoa* had been built in Pembroke Dockyard during the First World War and in the 1930s played the part of a German battle cruiser in the film *Brown on Resolution*. Cut in half by the *Queen Mary*, the *Curacoa* went quickly to the bottom and 338 men lost their lives.

A British gun crew at work.

November

Officers in the wheel house of a convoy escort plot the course.

The US ship building programme in full flow, with a new freighter on the stocks.

Rescuing airmen who had been shot down and the crews of sunken merchantmen was an unheralded but vital part of the war effort. This photograph shows RAF Air Sea Rescue launches in the English Channel.

Naval vessels supporting the Torch Landings.

An Allied convoy bound for North Africa, part of Operation Torch.

Landing artillery weapons as part of Operation Torch.

Admiral Cunningham, the man in command of the naval force during Operation Torch.

H.M.S. "Manxman".

Although officially rated as a mine layer, the *Manxman* was used in a variety of roles during the war. One of her most important functions was to make fast runs to help supply Malta.

On 17 November, Admiral Sir Max Horton was appointed C-in-C of the Western Approaches. He succeeded Percy Noble.

On 25 November, the submarine *Unshaken* lost her captain and her chief yeoman off the bridge during heavy weather. It was an unfortunate accident but it showed the perilous nature of operating submarines in bad weather.

On 27 November, as part of taking control of Vichy France, the Germans attempted to capture the Vichy fleet, then based at Toulon. Rather than allow their ships to fall into German hands, the French sailors promptly scuttled their ships.

French ships scuttled by their crews at Toulon.

An aerial view of the scuttled ships in Toulon harbour. The *Strasbourg* lies on the extreme right of the photograph.

The scuttling of the Toulon fleet proved to the British and French alike that the attack on French ships at Mers-el-Kebir in 1940 had been a disastrous operation which had done little more than sour Anglo-French relations.

The battleship *King George V.*

The carrier *Argus,* little more than a floating flight deck.

The old American four-stacker USS *Meade*, commissioned into the Royal Navy as HMS *Wells*.

Winston Churchill, who as well as being Prime Minister was also Minister of Defence, poses with his Chiefs of Staff in the garden at No. 10 Downing Street. Included among them is Admiral Sir Andrew Cunningham, the most successful British sailor of the war.

December

Operation Frankton was the official name for what has now become known as the story of the Cockleshell Heroes. This commando raid under the command of 'Blondie' Haslar was intended to destroy ships in the German-held port of Bordeaux. Six canoes were taken by submarine to the Gironde estuary, where they were launched and paddled ashore by the Marines.

Five ships were damaged
in the raid but only
two men, Haslar and
his partner Bill Sparks,
survived. The others were
either executed or died in
the expedition.

Unloading supplies by night in Malta, a difficult process but safer as far as aerial attack was concerned.

HMS *Euryalus* passes through the Suez Canal.

Sunderland in flight.

This photograph shows a two-man human torpedo coming to the surface. Such weapons were well used by the Italians, in particular, but Britain also employed them in various operations.

A British midget submarine on the surface. There is no conning tower and the officer taking bearings is strapped to the periscope stanchion to prevent him being swept overboard.

The destroyer *Achates* was lost in action against the *Admiral Hipper* when the German heavy cruiser and a number of destroyers attacked convoy JW 51B in the Barents Sea on 31 December. *Achates* was the last of forty-six British destroyers sunk during 1942.